Demystifying Large Language Models with Examples

Contents

Part 1: Unveiling the LLM Landscape

Chapter 1: Introduction to Large Language Models

Welcome to the fascinating world of Large Language Models (LLMs)! This chapter will equip you with the fundamentals of these powerful AI systems.

- **What are LLMs and how do they work?**

Imagine a computer program that can not only understand human language but also use it in remarkable ways. That's the essence of an LLM. These AI models are trained on massive amounts of text data, allowing them to grasp the nuances of language and perform various tasks. Think of them as super-powered language learners, constantly getting better at reading, writing, and even generating human-quality text.

But how do they achieve this magic? LLMs typically rely on a deep learning architecture called transformers. These are complex algorithms that analyze text data, identifying patterns and relationships between words. By processing massive amounts of text, LLMs learn the intricate web of language, enabling them to perform various tasks like writing different kinds of creative content, translating languages, or even summarizing complex information.

- **A Brief History of LLM Development**

The idea of machines understanding human language has captivated scientists for decades. The journey of LLMs began with simpler models, gradually evolving into the sophisticated systems we see today. The past decade has witnessed a significant acceleration in LLM development, fueled by the availability of immense datasets and advancements in computing power. Pioneering research institutions and companies like Google AI, OpenAI, and IBM have been at the forefront of pushing the boundaries of LLM capabilities.

- **Why Are LLMs Significant?**

LLMs hold immense potential to revolutionize how we interact with machines and information. Their ability to understand and generate human-like language opens doors to exciting possibilities across various fields. Imagine chatbots that can hold natural conversations, AI assistants that can write compelling marketing copy, or language translation tools that break down communication barriers. LLMs are poised to become powerful tools for enhancing creativity, streamlining communication, and unlocking new avenues for scientific exploration.

Chapter 2: Understanding the LLM Ecosystem

The LLM landscape is brimming with innovation. Let's delve deeper into the key players and technologies shaping this exciting field.

- **Key Players: Major Companies and Research Institutions Developing LLMs**

The development of LLMs is driven by a vibrant ecosystem of companies and research institutions.

Leading tech giants like Google, Microsoft, and Facebook are heavily invested in LLM research, pushing the boundaries of what these models can achieve. Renowned research institutions like MIT and Stanford are also at the forefront, contributing groundbreaking advancements in LLM architecture and training techniques.

- **Different LLM Architectures (e.g., Transformers)**

As mentioned earlier, transformers are the dominant architecture powering most advanced LLMs. These complex neural networks excel at analyzing sequential data like text. By focusing on specific parts of the input text (think of it as paying close attention during a conversation), transformers can effectively capture the context and relationships between words.

However, it's important to note that transformers are just one type of architecture. Researchers are constantly exploring new and innovative approaches to push the capabilities of LLMs even further.

- **Exploring Popular LLM Platforms (e.g., OpenAI API, Google AI)**

The good news is that you don't need to be an AI expert to leverage the power of LLMs. Several companies offer user-friendly platforms that allow you to interact with these models through APIs (Application Programming Interfaces). OpenAI API is a prominent example, providing access to powerful LLMs like GPT-3 for tasks like text generation and translation. Similarly, Google AI offers various LLM-powered tools through its cloud platform, enabling developers to integrate these capabilities into their applications.

By understanding the key players, architectures, and platforms, you'll gain a solid foundation for exploring the vast potential of LLMs in the chapters to come.

Part 2: LLMs in Action: A Compendium of Examples

Chapter 3: LLMs Unleashing Creativity: A Text Generation Playground

LLMs aren't just about analyzing information; they can also be incredibly creative partners. This chapter dives into how LLMs are transforming text generation across various domains.

- **A Muse for Creative Minds: Poems, Code, Scripts, and Musical Pieces**

Imagine having a collaborator who can brainstorm ideas, generate different creative text formats, and even adapt to your style. LLMs are making this a reality!

- **Poetry in Motion:** Prompt an LLM with a theme or starting line, and watch it weave words into a poem. You can even specify the style (e.g., haiku, sonnet) for a truly unique composition. Here's an example:

Input: Write a haiku about a cat basking in the sun.

Output: Golden fur aglow, Sun-drenched purrs fill the afternoon, Sleepy contentment.

- **Coding Companions:** LLMs can assist programmers by generating code snippets, completing functions, or even translating natural language instructions into code. For instance, you could describe the desired functionality of a program, and the LLM might generate the basic code structure to get you started.

- **Scriptwriting Support:** Struggling with writer's block for your next screenplay? LLMs can help develop dialogue, suggest plot points, or even create character descriptions based on your initial ideas.

- **Musical Masterminds (of sorts):** While composing a complete symphony might be a stretch, LLMs can generate musical pieces in a particular style or mood. Imagine feeding the LLM information about a genre and getting a melody as a starting point for your musical creation.

- **Content Creation Powerhouse: Blog Posts, Marketing Copy, Product Descriptions**

LLMs are becoming a valuable asset for content creators. They can help with:

- **Blog Brainstorming:** Provide a topic, and the LLM can generate outlines, suggest headlines, or even draft introductory paragraphs.

- **Marketing Magic:** Crafting compelling marketing copy can be time-consuming. LLMs can help by generating different ad variations or product descriptions tailored to specific audiences.

- **Product Description Dynamo:** No more writer's block for product descriptions! LLMs can generate clear and informative descriptions based on product features and specifications. Here's an example:

Input: Create a product description for a wireless noise-canceling headphone.

Output: Immerse yourself in crystal-clear audio with our wireless noise-canceling headphones. Featuring active noise cancellation technology, these headphones block out ambient distractions, letting you focus on your music, movies, or calls. Experience superior sound quality with powerful drivers and enjoy the freedom of wireless listening.

- **Different LLM Text Generation Techniques: Steering the Creative Flow**

While LLMs are impressive, they don't operate in a black box. Here are some ways to influence the text generation process:

- **Providing Prompts and Instructions:** The clearer your instructions, the better the LLM can tailor the output to your needs.
- **Setting the Style and Tone:** Want a funny blog post or a formal product description? Specify the desired style for a more targeted outcome.

- **Fine-Tuning with Examples:** If you have specific content examples you like, you can "fine-tune" the LLM to generate similar text formats.

By understanding these techniques, you can become an expert LLM collaborator, unlocking new levels of creativity in your text generation endeavors.

Chapter 4: LLMs Powering Conversations: From Chatbots to Clear Communication

LLMs are transforming the way we interact with machines and information. This chapter explores how LLMs are revolutionizing communication and interaction.

- **Chatbots and Virtual Assistants: Your Conversational Companions**

Imagine having a digital assistant that can answer your questions, complete tasks, or even have a casual chat. Chatbots powered by LLMs are making this a reality. These chatbots can be integrated into websites, messaging apps, or even smart devices, providing a convenient and interactive way to get things done.

- **Building an LLM-powered Chatbot: A Step-by-Step Example**

Let's get hands-on! Here's a simplified breakdown of how you could build a basic LLM-powered chatbot:

1. **Choose your LLM platform:** Several platforms offer access to LLMs through APIs (e.g., OpenAI API, Google Dialogflow).

2. **Train the LLM:** Provide the LLM with training data relevant to your chatbot's purpose. This could include conversation transcripts, FAQs, or specific domain knowledge.

3. **Design the conversation flow:** Define how the chatbot will respond to different user queries. This might involve setting up decision trees or using natural language understanding techniques.

4. **Integrate the LLM:** Connect your chatbot interface to the LLM platform, allowing the

chatbot to access the LLM's capabilities for real-time conversation generation.

This is a simplified view, but it highlights the potential of LLMs in creating more engaging and informative chatbots.

- **Machine Translation: Breaking Down Language Barriers**

LLMs are revolutionizing machine translation. By analyzing vast amounts of translated text, they can learn the nuances of different languages and generate more accurate and natural-sounding translations. Imagine effortlessly communicating with people worldwide or seamlessly accessing information in different languages.

- **Examples of LLM Translation Tasks:**

  - Translating news articles from one language to another.

  - Real-time conversation translation during video calls.

  - Localizing websites and marketing materials for a global audience.

- **Summarization and Paraphrasing Text: Extracting the Essence**

Ever felt overwhelmed by lengthy documents or articles? LLMs can condense information by creating summaries or paraphrases. This can save you time and help you grasp the key points of complex texts.

- **Examples of LLM Summaries:**

  o Summarizing research papers for a
    scientific review.

  o Creating concise summaries of news
    articles for a daily briefing.

  o Generating bullet point summaries of
    lengthy legal documents.

**Chapter 5: LLMs: Coding Companions for
Programmers**

LLMs are not just for wordsmiths; they can be a programmer's best friend as well. Here's how LLMs are transforming the world of code.

- **Code Generation and Completion: Writing Code Like a Pro (with a little LLM help)**

Imagine an AI assistant that can suggest code snippets, complete functions you've started, or even generate basic code structures based on your natural language description. LLMs are making this a reality, helping programmers write code faster and more efficiently.

- **Examples of Generating Code with LLMs:**
  - Automatically generating boilerplate code for common functionalities.

- Suggesting code completions as you type, similar to autocorrect for programmers.

- Translating natural language descriptions of desired program behavior into basic code structures.

- **Bug Detection and Fixing: LLMs as Debugging Detectives**

Finding and fixing bugs can be a time-consuming task for programmers. LLMs can analyze code and identify potential errors or inefficiencies. This can significantly reduce debugging time and improve code quality.

- **Demonstration of LLM-based code debugging:**

Imagine an LLM that can analyze your code and highlight potential issues based on its understanding of programming best practices and common error patterns. The LLM might even suggest potential fixes or point you towards relevant documentation to resolve the bug.

- **Automating Repetitive Coding Tasks: Freeing Up Time for Creative Work**

Many programming tasks are repetitive and time-consuming. LLMs can automate these tasks, freeing up programmers to focus on more creative and challenging aspects of software development.

- **Exploring an Example:**

Imagine an LLM that can automatically generate unit tests for your code, a task that can be tedious but crucial for ensuring code quality. This allows programmers to focus on writing the core functionalities of the program.

By leveraging LLMs for code generation, debugging, and automation, programmers can become more productive and efficient.

Chapter 6: LLMs Empowering Research and Analysis: Unveiling Insights from Data

LLMs are not just for creative endeavors; they are transforming research and analysis by helping us make sense of vast amounts of information.

- **Data Analysis and Insights Generation: Unearthing Hidden Gems**

Researchers and data analysts are bombarded with data. LLMs can analyze this data, identify patterns, and generate insights that might be difficult for humans to spot. Imagine sifting through mountains of customer data and the LLM automatically highlighting trends or correlations that could inform marketing strategies.

- **Showcasing an Example:**

  Researchers studying climate change could use LLMs to analyze weather data from various sources. The LLM might identify previously unknown climate patterns or correlations between different environmental factors.

- **Scientific Question Answering and Literature Review: Your Intelligent Research Assistant**

Scientific research involves a lot of reading and review. LLMs can be trained on vast scientific literature databases. This allows them to answer research questions directly or identify relevant research papers for a specific topic.

- **Demonstration with Examples:**

    Imagine a researcher studying a new disease. They could use an LLM-powered system to query a database of medical journals for relevant research on similar diseases or specific genes associated with the illness. This can significantly accelerate the research process.

- **Exploring the Potential of LLMs in Drug Discovery:**

Drug discovery is a complex and time-consuming process. LLMs can analyze vast datasets of chemical compounds and biological information to identify potential drug candidates. This can expedite the discovery of new medications and treatments for various diseases.

- **Use Case Example:**

  Imagine an LLM trained on a massive database of known drugs and their chemical structures. Researchers could use this LLM to identify existing drugs that might be repurposed to treat a new disease based on their biological

properties.

By assisting with data analysis, scientific literature

review, and even drug discovery, LLMs are becoming

powerful tools for researchers and scientists across

various disciplines.

Exploring Transformer Architectures in Detail

Large Language Models (LLMs) are built on
sophisticated architectures that have revolutionized
natural language processing (NLP). Among these
architectures, the Transformer model stands out as
the cornerstone for most state-of-the-art language
models today, including GPT, BERT, and their
derivatives. This section delves deeply into
Transformer architectures, breaking down their
components, how they work, and why they are so

effective at handling complex tasks like text generation, summarization, translation, and even more intricate operations such as reasoning and decision-making.

The Transformer model was introduced by Vaswani et al. in the paper *Attention is All You Need*, published in 2017. Prior to the Transformer, many of the top-performing NLP models were built on recurrent neural networks (RNNs) and their advanced versions, Long Short-Term Memory (LSTM) networks. While LSTMs were able to model sequences of data by maintaining hidden states over time, they suffered from issues like vanishing gradients and inefficient parallelization. The Transformer eliminated these limitations by abandoning the recurrence mechanism entirely, focusing instead on self-attention and parallelization, allowing it to handle long-range dependencies more effectively.

The core idea behind the Transformer architecture is the self-attention mechanism. This mechanism enables the model to weigh the importance of each word in a sentence relative to all other words in the sentence, regardless of their distance from one another. Unlike traditional RNNs, which process the input sequentially, the Transformer processes all the words in the sentence simultaneously, allowing for more efficient learning and understanding of context.

Self-attention operates through a series of steps. For each word in a sentence, the model calculates three vectors: the *query*, the *key*, and the *value*. These vectors are derived from the word's embedding, and they are used to compute the attention score, which indicates the relevance of each word to the others in the sentence. The attention score is then used to weight the corresponding value vector, producing a weighted sum that represents the contextualized word.

To facilitate this, the Transformer is divided into two main components: the *encoder* and the *decoder*. Both components consist of a stack of identical layers. The encoder processes the input sequence, while the decoder generates the output sequence. The encoder and decoder are connected through attention mechanisms, which allow the decoder to focus on different parts of the input sequence at each step in the generation process.

A key feature of the Transformer is its ability to scale efficiently. Because the model processes all words in parallel rather than sequentially, it can take full advantage of modern hardware, such as GPUs and TPUs, to speed up training. Additionally, the attention mechanism itself is highly parallelizable, further enhancing the model's efficiency.

The Transformer is also designed to handle long-range dependencies between words, which was a major challenge for earlier models like RNNs. The self-attention mechanism allows each word to attend to every other word in the sequence, regardless of distance. This makes the model highly effective at understanding complex linguistic structures and context over long sequences of text.

However, while the Transformer architecture offers many advantages, it also presents some challenges. One of the primary concerns is its computational complexity. The attention mechanism requires a matrix multiplication between the query and key vectors, which can be costly in terms of memory and computation, especially for long sequences. This has led to the development of various optimizations and approximations, such as sparse attention and efficient transformers, which aim to reduce the computational burden without sacrificing performance.

Despite these challenges, the Transformer has become the foundation for most state-of-the-art LLMs. By understanding how self-attention works and how the Transformer is structured, we can better appreciate the advancements in NLP that have come as a result of this architecture. The next step in LLM development involves fine-tuning the model on domain-specific data and optimizing it for particular tasks, which requires a deep understanding of training strategies and model evaluation techniques.

Understanding Attention Mechanisms Beyond Self-Attention

The self-attention mechanism, which underpins Transformer architectures, is not only crucial for understanding context within sequences of text but also serves as the foundation for a variety of more advanced attention mechanisms in modern LLMs. While self-attention operates within a single sequence, enabling the model to capture the relationships between words, additional forms of attention can extend this capability and enhance a model's flexibility and performance.

Multi-head attention is one such extension of self-attention. This technique involves using multiple attention heads that each focus on different parts of the input sequence. Each attention head computes its own set of attention scores, which are then concatenated and passed through a linear layer to form the final output. The idea behind multi-head attention is to allow the model to attend to different subspaces of the input data, capturing a richer representation of the input than any single attention head could. For instance, one attention head might focus on syntactic relations, while another focuses on semantic ones. This helps LLMs learn more complex patterns and dependencies across multiple levels of abstraction in the input sequence.

In practice, multi-head attention has been found to significantly improve the ability of models like GPT and BERT to understand and generate nuanced language, enabling them to tackle tasks that require a deep understanding of context, such as text summarization, translation, and dialogue generation. Moreover, the scalability of this approach, in conjunction with the parallelization benefits of the Transformer, has made it a cornerstone for handling large datasets and improving the generalization capabilities of LLMs.

Other attention variants, such as cross-attention and sparse attention, are also increasingly important. Cross-attention is typically used in the context of sequence-to-sequence models, where the decoder uses it to attend to the encoder's output. This type of attention is useful in tasks like machine translation, where the model needs to generate a target sequence based on an input sequence from a different language.

Sparse attention, on the other hand, is a key research area designed to mitigate the computational inefficiency of full self-attention. In sparse attention models, only a subset of the attention scores are computed, focusing on the most relevant parts of the input sequence. This approach reduces the memory and computational requirements, making it viable to scale attention mechanisms to much longer sequences, an ongoing challenge in LLM development.

These advanced attention mechanisms are not only improving the performance of LLMs but are also helping to make them more efficient, thereby driving further advancements in language modeling and other AI applications.

Training LLMs: From Data to Model Convergence

Training Large Language Models involves a highly complex and resource-intensive process. Unlike smaller machine learning models, LLMs require massive datasets, powerful hardware infrastructure, and carefully designed training procedures to achieve high performance. The process of training an LLM can be broken down into several stages, each of which presents unique challenges and considerations.

The first and most crucial step in training LLMs is data collection and curation. The quality and quantity of data used to train an LLM can significantly impact its performance. LLMs require vast amounts of text data, typically spanning multiple domains and languages, to learn the intricacies of language. Sourcing diverse datasets from the web, academic papers, books, and even proprietary data is essential for ensuring that the model captures a broad spectrum of linguistic patterns.

Once the data is gathered, preprocessing is the next critical step. Text data often needs to be cleaned and normalized to ensure consistency across the entire dataset. This involves tokenizing the text, converting it into a standardized format, and handling issues like spelling variations, punctuation differences, and grammatical inconsistencies. For example, certain words might appear in multiple forms (e.g., "color" vs. "colour"), and the model needs to recognize them as the same entity.

Training LLMs typically involves two primary phases: pre-training and fine-tuning. In the pre-training phase, the model learns general language patterns through unsupervised learning. This stage involves training the model on a large corpus of text to predict the next word or sentence, capturing high-level structures and contextual relationships. For instance, GPT-based models use a causal language modeling objective, where the model predicts the next word in a sequence based on the previous words. This pre-training allows the model to build a rich understanding of syntax, grammar, and semantic relationships.

The fine-tuning phase is where domain-specific knowledge is introduced. This phase usually involves supervised learning, where the model is trained on a more targeted dataset that is relevant to a specific application, such as medical text or legal documents. Fine-tuning adjusts the model's parameters to make it more suitable for particular tasks like question answering, classification, or summarization.

One of the primary challenges in training LLMs is achieving model convergence. Convergence refers to the point where the model's performance stabilizes, and further training does not result in significant improvements. Ensuring convergence requires careful monitoring of the loss function, a measure of how well the model is performing on the training data. If the model overfits to the training data or underfits, adjustments to the learning rate, batch size, or model architecture may be necessary.

Training large models can also be computationally expensive. High-end hardware like GPUs and TPUs is often required to accelerate training, and models like GPT-3, with 175 billion parameters, require a substantial amount of memory and processing power. Strategies like distributed training, where the model is trained across multiple machines, and mixed-precision training, which uses lower-precision calculations to speed up training without sacrificing accuracy, are commonly employed to tackle these challenges.

Fine-Tuning LLMs: Tailoring to Specific Tasks

Once a Large Language Model has been pre-trained on a general corpus, it often needs to be fine-tuned for specific tasks. Fine-tuning allows a model to adapt its pre-trained knowledge to solve specialized problems, making it more effective for real-world applications. This section explores the techniques, strategies, and considerations for fine-tuning LLMs, focusing on task-specific performance improvement.

The fine-tuning process typically involves training the model on a smaller, task-specific dataset. The key difference between pre-training and fine-tuning is the data used and the objective of training. In pre-training, the objective is to learn general language patterns, whereas in fine-tuning, the model learns to optimize for a specific objective, such as text classification, named entity recognition, or sentiment analysis.

One of the most important decisions when fine-tuning an LLM is the selection of the dataset. The dataset should closely resemble the kind of text the model will encounter in production. For example, if the goal is to create a model for medical text, the fine-tuning dataset should include clinical reports, research papers, and medical textbooks. Fine-tuning on domain-specific data helps the model learn the specialized vocabulary and domain-specific knowledge required to perform well in that area.

Another critical aspect of fine-tuning is choosing the appropriate training objective. While LLMs like GPT use causal language modeling, other LLMs like BERT employ a masked language modeling objective, where a portion of the input text is masked, and the model is tasked with predicting the missing parts. Depending on the task, the training objective may need to be adjusted. For example, in a question-answering task, the model may be trained to predict an answer span within a passage of text, while in a sentiment analysis task, the model may predict the sentiment of a given sentence.

Fine-tuning can be done in a few different ways, depending on the task and the model's architecture. One common method is full model fine-tuning, where all the parameters of the model are updated during training. However, this can be computationally expensive and time-consuming. Another method is called "adapter tuning," where small modules (adapters) are added to the model and fine-tuned instead of the entire network. This allows for efficient fine-tuning, as the base model remains frozen, and only a small number of additional parameters are trained.

One challenge during fine-tuning is catastrophic forgetting, where the model forgets the knowledge it learned during pre-training when it adapts to the new task. To address this, techniques like gradual unfreezing, in which layers of the model are gradually unfrozen for fine-tuning, can help prevent significant forgetting. Additionally, methods like knowledge distillation, where a smaller model learns from the outputs of the larger pre-trained model, can be used to retain the general knowledge learned during pre-

training while allowing for task-specific fine-tuning.

Scaling Large Language Models: Techniques and Trade-offs

Scaling Large Language Models to handle increasingly

complex tasks and larger datasets requires careful

consideration of multiple factors, including

computational efficiency, model size, and data throughput. As the size of models continues to grow, the challenges associated with training, deploying, and optimizing them also increase. This section discusses the strategies for scaling LLMs, the trade-offs involved, and the emerging techniques that enable the development of larger and more capable models.

One of the most significant trends in LLM development is the increase in model size. Models like GPT-3, with 175 billion parameters, and newer models like GPT-4 are pushing the boundaries of what is possible with current hardware. However, as model size grows, so do the computational and memory requirements. Training large models can take weeks or even months on the most advanced supercomputing infrastructure, and even inference can be slow and costly.

To address these challenges, several techniques have been developed to optimize the scalability of LLMs. One such technique is model parallelism, where a large model is split across multiple devices, with each device handling a different part of the model. This allows the model to scale beyond the memory limitations of a single machine, but it introduces complexity in managing inter-device communication.

Another technique is pipeline parallelism, where the model is divided into several stages, and each stage is processed on a different machine. This allows for better load balancing and helps to reduce idle time, making it more efficient to scale large models.

Beyond parallelism, approaches like mixed-precision training are crucial for improving the efficiency of large-scale model training. Mixed-precision training reduces memory usage by utilizing lower-precision (e.g., 16-bit) floating-point arithmetic instead of the standard 32-bit precision. This speeds up training and reduces memory usage, allowing larger models to be trained on the same hardware.

However, scaling up comes with trade-offs. One of the key trade-offs is the cost of training and inference. As model size increases, so do the computational costs, making it expensive to train large models. Techniques like model pruning, where less important weights are removed, can help mitigate this cost, but they may come at the expense of performance. Additionally, large models are more prone to overfitting, which can reduce their generalization ability and lead to poorer performance on unseen data.

Despite these challenges, scaling LLMs has led to significant breakthroughs in natural language understanding and generation, enabling models to perform tasks that were once thought impossible, such as generating coherent long-form text, answering complex questions, and engaging in meaningful conversations.

Optimizing Large Language Models: Hyperparameters

and Beyond

Hyperparameter tuning is a critical step in the process

of optimizing large language models (LLMs). While

these models are typically pre-trained on vast

amounts of data, the performance of the model can

be greatly improved through careful optimization of

hyperparameters. The process of hyperparameter tuning involves selecting the best combination of model parameters that lead to the highest performance on a specific task.

In LLMs, key hyperparameters include the learning rate, batch size, number of layers, number of attention heads, and the size of the hidden layers. Each of these parameters has a direct impact on the model's training process and its ability to generalize. For example, too high of a learning rate can lead to unstable training, while too low of a learning rate can result in slow convergence.

Grid search and random search are the most basic methods for hyperparameter tuning. However, more advanced techniques like Bayesian optimization and population-based training have become popular for tuning hyperparameters in LLMs. Bayesian optimization uses a probabilistic model to predict the performance of different hyperparameter configurations and iteratively refines the search space, making it a more efficient approach than grid search.

In addition to hyperparameter tuning, techniques like regularization and early stopping can be used to improve the generalization ability of LLMs. Regularization techniques such as dropout and weight decay help prevent overfitting, while early stopping monitors the validation loss during training and halts training once the model stops improving on the validation set.

Optimizing LLMs is an ongoing challenge that requires balancing performance with computational efficiency. As models become more complex and data-intensive, new techniques and tools will continue to emerge to help manage and optimize these large models effectively.

Advanced Regularization Techniques for LLMs

Regularization is a crucial component of training large language models (LLMs), particularly as these models scale in size and complexity. Large models are inherently more prone to overfitting due to their vast number of parameters, which can memorize training

data rather than generalize to unseen examples.
Regularization techniques help mitigate this issue,
ensuring that the model performs well on new,
unseen data while retaining its ability to capture
general patterns.

One of the most common regularization techniques in
LLMs is **Dropout**. Dropout randomly disables a
fraction of the model's neurons during training,
forcing the network to learn redundant
representations of data and improving its ability to
generalize. Dropout is particularly effective in
preventing co-adaptation of neurons, where neurons
become overly reliant on each other, potentially
leading to overfitting. The key challenge with dropout

is choosing the optimal rate, as a rate that is too high can prevent the model from learning effectively.

Another widely used technique is **Weight Decay**, also known as L2 regularization. Weight decay penalizes large weights during training, which discourages the model from relying too heavily on individual features. This results in a smoother, more generalizable model that doesn't overfit to noise in the training data. Weight decay is often used in conjunction with other techniques like Adam optimization to fine-tune the model's weight updates.

Early Stopping is another important regularization method that can prevent overfitting during the training process. Early stopping monitors the model's performance on a validation set and halts training when the validation loss begins to increase, indicating that the model is starting to overfit to the training data. This method is particularly useful when training large models on vast datasets, as it can save computational resources and reduce unnecessary overfitting.

More advanced regularization methods like **Label Smoothing** can be particularly effective in classification tasks. Label smoothing modifies the target labels during training, replacing hard targets (e.g., 0 or 1) with softer, probabilistic targets. This technique helps prevent the model from becoming overly confident about its predictions, encouraging it to maintain a degree of uncertainty, which can improve generalization.

Finally, **Data Augmentation** is also a key regularization strategy. By artificially expanding the training dataset through various transformations (e.g., synonym replacement, back-translation, paraphrasing), the model is exposed to a wider variety of inputs and can learn more robust features. This is particularly effective in NLP tasks such as text classification, sentiment analysis, and question answering, where data diversity can enhance the model's ability to generalize across different domains.

Fine-Tuning LLMs for Multimodal Tasks

Fine-tuning large language models (LLMs) for **multimodal tasks**—those that require understanding and generating multiple types of data, such as text, images, and sound—has become a key frontier in AI research. Multimodal models enable the integration of various data modalities, creating models that can process and generate both textual and non-textual data. This capability is especially important for applications like image captioning, video analysis, and multimodal search engines, where different types of input need to be processed simultaneously.

In multimodal LLMs, **transformers** are typically used to model both text and non-text data, due to their flexibility in handling various data formats. A common architecture for such tasks is the **Vision Transformer (ViT)**, which can be combined with language models to create hybrid architectures. The model is trained to process images and text in parallel, with shared parameters between the modalities. For example, in image captioning, the model takes an image as input, generates an embedding through a vision model, and uses that embedding to produce a textual description through the language model.

Fine-tuning multimodal models involves using datasets that contain paired data, such as image-text pairs. One popular approach for fine-tuning in this domain is **cross-attention**. Cross-attention allows a model to focus on both the visual features of an image and the semantic features of a text sequence simultaneously, generating a unified representation of both. For example, when generating captions for images, the model learns to pay attention to both the objects in the image and the context provided by the text.

Another technique for fine-tuning multimodal models is **modal-specific embeddings**. In this approach, each modality (e.g., text, image, sound) is processed through a specialized network that generates embeddings. These embeddings are then fused into a shared space where the model can learn interactions between the modalities. The benefit of this technique is that it allows the model to retain modality-specific features while learning cross-modal representations.

A key challenge in fine-tuning multimodal LLMs is **alignment**—ensuring that the representations learned from different modalities are properly aligned so that the model can effectively map between them. This requires careful handling of the fusion process, as poorly aligned representations can degrade model performance, especially in tasks like video captioning, where both temporal and spatial alignment of modalities are critical.

Moreover, the size of multimodal models can be computationally intensive, requiring careful optimization. Techniques like **knowledge distillation** (where a smaller model is trained to mimic the behavior of a larger model) and **pruning** can help reduce the computational load of multimodal models while maintaining high accuracy.

Scaling LLMs Efficiently with Distributed Training

As the size of large language models (LLMs) continues to increase, the computational requirements to train them also scale exponentially. The ability to efficiently train LLMs on large-scale datasets is critical for pushing the boundaries of AI. Distributed training has become the go-to solution for scaling up LLMs, enabling the training of models that would otherwise be impossible to train on a single machine.

Data Parallelism is one of the primary methods of distributed training. In this approach, the training dataset is split across multiple devices (e.g., GPUs or TPUs). Each device processes a different portion of the data, and the model weights are updated based on the gradients computed from the local data on each device. The gradients from each device are then averaged (or summed) and used to update the global model parameters. This approach is highly scalable and efficient, as it allows for simultaneous processing of large datasets across multiple devices.

Model Parallelism is another strategy used in distributed training, particularly for very large models that cannot fit into the memory of a single device. In model parallelism, the model itself is split across multiple devices, with each device responsible for different parts of the model. For instance, one device might handle the first few layers of the model, while another device handles the remaining layers. The output from one device is passed as input to the next device. This technique can be challenging to implement due to the overhead of communication between devices, but it allows for the training of models that exceed the memory capacity of individual devices.

Pipeline Parallelism combines elements of both data and model parallelism. In this approach, the model is divided into stages (e.g., layers), and each stage is assigned to a different device. The training data is processed in a pipeline, with different batches of data passed through the various stages of the model in parallel. Pipeline parallelism allows for more efficient use of available hardware, as each device can continuously process different batches of data while performing different stages of computation.

To optimize distributed training, **gradient accumulation** is often used. In distributed training setups with smaller batch sizes, gradient accumulation allows multiple forward passes to be accumulated before updating the weights. This technique can help stabilize training and improve convergence, especially when the batch size is constrained by the hardware.

Distributed training is not without its challenges. The primary concern is **communication overhead**, especially when the model is spread across many devices. Techniques like **model sharding**, where the model weights are partitioned into smaller pieces and distributed more efficiently, and **asynchronous gradient updates**, where updates are made without waiting for synchronization across devices, help

mitigate these issues. Additionally, recent

developments in **mixed-precision training** allow for

faster training and reduced memory usage by using

lower-precision arithmetic during training.

Managing and Deploying LLMs at Scale

Deploying large language models (LLMs) in production

environments presents a unique set of challenges.

These models often require significant computational

resources for inference, and their size can make them

difficult to deploy on a single server. Managing LLMs

at scale requires strategies for optimizing their

performance, reducing latency, and ensuring they can handle large volumes of requests in real-time.

One of the primary challenges of deploying LLMs is **inference latency**. Large models, particularly those with billions of parameters, can take considerable time to generate predictions. Reducing this latency is crucial for applications like conversational agents or real-time text generation, where responsiveness is key. Techniques such as **quantization**, where the precision of the model weights is reduced, can help reduce inference time by making the model more lightweight without sacrificing too much accuracy. **Distillation**, where a smaller, more efficient model is trained to replicate the behavior of a larger model, can also be used to speed up inference while maintaining the core capabilities of the original model.

Another important consideration is **model serving**. Large models typically require specialized infrastructure to be served efficiently in production. Tools like **TensorFlow Serving**, **TorchServe**, and **NVIDIA Triton** are designed to deploy machine learning models at scale, providing features like batching, multi-model support, and optimized inference. For instance, **batching** allows multiple requests to be processed in parallel, reducing the overhead associated with individual requests and improving overall throughput.

When deploying LLMs, **scaling the infrastructure** to handle high traffic volumes is crucial. One approach to scaling is **containerization**, using tools like Docker and Kubernetes to package the model and its dependencies into portable containers. This allows for easy deployment across different environments and ensures that the model can be replicated and scaled horizontally across multiple servers.

To further enhance scalability, **serverless architectures** can be used, where models are deployed on-demand and scaled automatically based on traffic. Services like AWS Lambda and Google Cloud Functions allow for auto-scaling, where resources are provisioned dynamically based on incoming requests, ensuring optimal performance during peak demand.

Finally, monitoring and **model versioning** are key to maintaining a deployed model. Regularly monitoring the model's performance on real-world data allows teams to detect issues like model drift (where the model's accuracy decreases over time due to changes in data distributions) and take corrective action. Versioning helps ensure that updates to the model don't disrupt service and allows for easy rollback if an update introduces issues.

Optimizing Energy Consumption for LLM Training and Deployment

As large language models (LLMs) grow in size and complexity, their energy consumption has become a significant concern. Training and deploying these models can be computationally expensive and energy-intensive, raising both environmental and cost-related challenges. Addressing these concerns requires a combination of optimization strategies and innovations in both hardware and software.

One approach to improving energy efficiency is **energy-efficient hardware**. Graphics Processing Units (GPUs) and Tensor Processing Units (TPUs) are designed to handle the parallel nature of LLM computations. However, as these devices become more powerful, they also consume more power. Choosing the right hardware for LLM tasks is crucial in minimizing energy use without sacrificing performance. Companies like NVIDIA and Google are continuously working to improve the energy efficiency of their AI-specific hardware, offering options that strike a balance between speed and power consumption.

In addition to hardware, **software optimizations** can also reduce the energy footprint of LLMs. One method is **mixed-precision training**, which reduces the computational load by using lower-precision arithmetic, requiring less energy and memory.

Similarly, **model pruning**, where redundant or less important weights are removed, can help create smaller models that require less power to train and serve, without significantly compromising performance.

Another technique to reduce energy consumption is **gradient checkpointing**, a memory optimization method that reduces the need to store all intermediate activations during the forward pass. This reduces memory usage and, by extension, energy consumption. It also enables training larger models on limited hardware, potentially lowering the overall computational cost.

On the deployment side, **energy-efficient inference** techniques, such as batching and model distillation, can significantly reduce the computational resources required for serving models in production. Reducing the complexity of models for inference, for example through quantization or distillation, can result in faster, less energy-consuming predictions.

Finally, **carbon offsetting** initiatives and utilizing renewable energy sources for training and deployment can help mitigate the environmental impact of LLM training. Many cloud providers offer services that are powered by renewable energy, which can reduce the carbon footprint associated with large-scale AI model development.

Part 3: The Future of LLMs: Charting an Uncharted

Course

Chapter 7: Challenges and Ethical Considerations of

LLMs: Walking the Tightrope

LLMs hold immense potential, but like any powerful technology, they come with their own set of challenges. This chapter explores some key ethical considerations that need to be addressed as LLMs become more integrated into our lives.

- **Bias and Fairness in LLM Outputs: Ensuring Equitable Treatment**

LLMs are trained on massive datasets of text and code, which can reflect the biases present in the real world. This can lead to biased outputs, potentially perpetuating discrimination or unfair treatment. We need to be vigilant about identifying and mitigating bias in LLM development and deployment.

- **Exploring Potential Biases:**

Imagine an LLM trained on a dataset of news articles that primarily feature men in leadership roles. This LLM might be more likely to generate text that reinforces gender stereotypes. It's crucial to identify and address such biases to ensure fair and inclusive outcomes.

- **Explainability and Interpretability of LLM Decisions: Understanding the Why Behind the What**

LLMs are complex AI systems, and their decision-making processes can be opaque. This lack of explainability can be problematic, making it difficult to understand how and why an LLM arrives at a particular output.

- **The Importance of Explainability:**

  Imagine an LLM used in a loan application process that rejects a loan request. Without understanding the LLM's reasoning, it's difficult to assess the fairness of the decision. Developing more transparent LLMs will be crucial for building trust and ensuring responsible AI practices.

- **Security and Privacy Concerns with LLMs: Protecting Sensitive Information**

LLMs trained on vast amounts of data raise privacy concerns. It's crucial to ensure that sensitive information is not inadvertently leaked through LLM outputs. Additionally, security measures need to be in place to prevent malicious actors from exploiting LLMs for disinformation or other harmful purposes.

By acknowledging these challenges and proactively addressing them, we can ensure that LLMs are developed and used ethically, promoting fairness, transparency, and responsible AI practices.

Chapter 8: The LLM Revolution: Reshaping Industries

LLMs are poised to disrupt various industries,

transforming the way we work, learn, and interact

with technology. This chapter explores some potential

applications across different sectors.

- **Education and Training: Personalized Learning**
  Experiences

LLMs can personalize the learning experience by

tailoring educational materials and assessments to

individual student needs. Imagine an LLM-powered

tutor that can provide targeted feedback and suggest learning resources based on a student's strengths and weaknesses.

- **Customer Service and Marketing: Enhanced Engagement and Personalization**

LLMs can power chatbots that can handle customer inquiries more effectively, providing 24/7 support and personalized recommendations. Marketing campaigns can be optimized using LLMs to generate targeted content and predict customer behavior.

- **Demonstrating Use Cases:**
  - An LLM-powered chatbot in a retail store can answer customer questions about product features and availability.

- An LLM can analyze customer data to identify buying patterns and personalize marketing campaigns for different customer segments.

- **Creative Industries: A Spark of Inspiration or the Future of Creativity?**

LLMs can assist creative professionals by generating ideas, writing different creative text formats, or even composing music pieces. However, the role of human creativity will still be crucial in shaping the final product.

- **Discussing the Impact on Creative Fields:**

Imagine a musician using an LLM to generate a melody as a starting point for a new song. The human artist would then use their creativity and skill to refine the melody and add their own musical style.

The impact of LLMs on the creative industries will likely be multifaceted, offering new tools and possibilities while also prompting discussions about the role of human creativity in the age of AI

Case Study 1: LLMs in Healthcare: Enhancing Clinical Decision Support Systems

Overview:

In the healthcare industry, LLMs are being used to improve clinical decision support systems (CDSS) by enabling more accurate diagnoses, treatment recommendations, and personalized care. The integration of LLMs into Electronic Health Records (EHR) systems allows healthcare professionals to access detailed patient information and receive AI-assisted insights, improving overall patient care.

Challenge:

Traditional CDSS faced several issues, such as inaccurate recommendations due to limited data, lack of contextual understanding, and inability to process vast amounts of unstructured data in patient records. While older systems relied on predefined rules, they failed to incorporate new knowledge, medical literature, and subtle patient details, limiting their effectiveness.

Implementation:

A major healthcare provider partnered with a leading AI company to develop an LLM-based CDSS. The system was integrated with the hospital's EHR platform to analyze both structured and unstructured data—such as medical histories, lab results, doctor's notes, and patient reports. By fine-tuning an LLM on a large corpus of medical texts, the system was able to process natural language inputs, extracting insights from clinical documents and medical journals in real-time.

Key steps involved:

1. **Data Collection**: The system was trained using a diverse dataset of clinical records, research papers, and drug interaction databases.

2. **Natural Language Processing (NLP)**: NLP techniques were used to extract meaningful patterns from unstructured data, like patient symptoms, previous treatments, and outcomes.

3. **Model Fine-Tuning**: An existing LLM, like GPT-3, was fine-tuned specifically on the medical corpus to understand medical terminology and nuances.

Outcome:

The integration of LLMs into the CDSS resulted in the following improvements:

1. **Enhanced Decision Making**: Healthcare professionals received more accurate and timely recommendations based on the latest medical literature and patient data.

2. **Reduced Errors**: The AI-driven system helped reduce diagnostic errors and treatment delays by providing real-time alerts and insights.

3. **Personalized Care**: The system could generate personalized treatment suggestions based on patient-specific data, optimizing care and improving outcomes.

4. **Improved Efficiency**: By automating data processing and analysis, the system freed up healthcare professionals to focus more on patient care.

Challenges and Solutions:

- **Data Privacy**: Given the sensitivity of healthcare data, the team implemented strict encryption protocols and ensured compliance with HIPAA regulations to safeguard patient information.

- **Model Transparency**: To address concerns about the black-box nature of AI, the system provided healthcare professionals with explanations of its decision-making process.

Conclusion:

The deployment of LLMs in the healthcare sector demonstrates the potential of AI in improving clinical decision-making and patient outcomes. The successful integration of LLMs into CDSS represents a significant

leap toward AI-assisted healthcare.

Case Study 2: LLMs in Finance: Automating Customer

Support and Financial Advisory Services

Overview:

The financial services industry has been leveraging

LLMs to automate customer service, risk analysis, and

financial advisory services. These applications help

banks and financial institutions enhance customer

experiences, reduce costs, and improve operational efficiency.

Challenge:

Financial institutions were facing challenges in handling high volumes of customer inquiries and providing personalized financial advice. Manual processing was resource-intensive and often led to delayed responses. Furthermore, the existing chatbots and automated systems lacked the ability to understand complex financial concepts and offer insightful recommendations.

Implementation:

A leading bank decided to implement an AI-driven chatbot based on a fine-tuned LLM to automate customer support and provide personalized financial advice. The LLM was trained on a dataset consisting of financial documents, customer queries, market trends, and investment strategies. The chatbot was integrated with the bank's CRM system and could access real-time account information, enabling it to answer queries, process transactions, and make personalized investment recommendations.

Key steps included:

1. **Data Collection**: The model was trained on a vast corpus of customer support logs, financial reports, and customer interaction histories to ensure it could handle a wide range of inquiries.

2. **Fine-Tuning**: The LLM was fine-tuned to understand financial terminology, customer sentiment, and context-specific language used in banking.

3. **Deployment**: The chatbot was deployed across multiple channels, including the bank's website, mobile app, and voice interfaces.

Outcome:

The implementation of the LLM-driven chatbot led to:

1. **Improved Customer Support**: The chatbot was able to handle routine customer inquiries 24/7, providing immediate responses to questions regarding account balances, transaction history, and loan eligibility.

2. **Personalized Financial Advice**: By analyzing customer data, the LLM could suggest personalized investment strategies, savings plans, and loan products tailored to the individual's financial goals and risk profile.

3. **Operational Efficiency**: The bank reduced operational costs by automating customer service and advisory functions, allowing human advisors to focus on more complex cases.

4. **Customer Satisfaction**: The chatbot's ability to provide instant, accurate responses improved customer satisfaction and engagement.

Challenges and Solutions:

- **Security and Compliance**: The bank ensured that the chatbot was compliant with financial regulations such as GDPR and PCI-DSS by implementing strict data security protocols.

- **Handling Complex Queries**: While the LLM performed well with routine queries, it struggled with more complex financial situations. To address this, the system was designed to escalate complex inquiries to human agents.

Conclusion:

LLMs are revolutionizing customer support and financial advisory services in the banking sector by automating routine tasks, providing personalized insights, and improving efficiency.

Case Study 3: LLMs in E-Commerce: Personalizing

Product Recommendations and Customer

Engagement

Overview:

In the e-commerce industry, personalized customer

experiences are crucial for driving sales and customer loyalty. By leveraging LLMs, e-commerce platforms are able to enhance product recommendations, improve customer engagement, and streamline customer support.

Challenge:

E-commerce platforms faced difficulties in offering highly personalized product recommendations, especially as they scaled. Traditional recommendation systems were based on collaborative filtering or rule-based algorithms, which often failed to capture complex customer preferences and seasonal trends. Additionally, customer service bots lacked the ability to engage in natural, context-aware conversations.

Implementation:

An online retail giant decided to incorporate LLMs into their recommendation engine and customer service systems. The recommendation system used an LLM to analyze past purchasing behavior, search queries, and product reviews to predict and suggest relevant products to customers. The customer service chatbot, powered by the same LLM, was designed to answer product-related queries, assist with order tracking, and provide personalized shopping assistance.

Key steps included:

1. **Data Collection**: The LLM was trained on a large corpus of product descriptions, customer reviews, and transaction histories.

2. **Personalization Algorithms**: The model incorporated customer preferences, buying patterns, and seasonality to deliver tailored recommendations.

3. **Natural Language Interaction**: The chatbot was trained to understand and respond to a wide range of customer queries in a conversational manner.

Outcome:

The results were as follows:

1. **Increased Sales**: Personalized recommendations led to higher conversion rates and average order value by presenting customers with

relevant products based on their individual tastes.

2. **Enhanced Customer Engagement**: The LLM-driven chatbot was able to provide real-time product recommendations, resolve inquiries, and offer personalized discounts, leading to greater customer engagement.

3. **Reduced Customer Support Costs**: The chatbot automated a significant portion of customer service interactions, reducing the need for human agents and lowering operational costs.

Challenges and Solutions:

- **Data Privacy**: The company ensured that customer data used for personalization was anonymized and stored securely to comply with privacy regulations.

- **Model Robustness**: The model occasionally struggled with new or niche products. To solve this, the team implemented hybrid recommendation methods that combined LLM-generated suggestions with collaborative filtering techniques.

Conclusion:

By integrating LLMs into their recommendation systems and customer service operations, e-commerce companies can provide highly personalized experiences that drive sales and customer satisfaction.

Case Study 4: LLMs in Legal Tech: Automating Document Review and Contract Analysis

Overview:

Legal technology (legal tech) is transforming how law firms and corporate legal departments manage contracts, compliance, and document review. LLMs are used to automate tedious and time-consuming tasks like contract analysis, legal research, and document categorization.

Challenge:

Law firms traditionally relied on manual processes for document review and legal research. These tasks were labor-intensive and time-consuming, often requiring lawyers to go through large volumes of documents to identify relevant clauses, precedents, or case law. This not only consumed significant resources but also increased the risk of human error.

Implementation:

A leading legal tech company developed an AI-powered tool that used LLMs to automate the analysis of legal documents, such as contracts and non-disclosure agreements (NDAs). The system was trained on a vast dataset of legal documents, including contracts, court rulings, and legal textbooks, to understand the structure and terminology of legal language.

Key steps included:

1. **Data Preparation**: The LLM was trained using a comprehensive dataset of legal contracts, case law, and statutes, ensuring that it could understand legal jargon and concepts.

2. **Contract Analysis**: The system was deployed to automatically review contracts and highlight key clauses, flag potential risks, and suggest revisions.

3. **Legal Research**: The LLM was integrated with a legal database to help lawyers find relevant case law, precedents, and statutes in response to specific legal queries.

Outcome:

The implementation of LLMs resulted in:

1. **Reduced Time for Document Review**: The automated system drastically reduced the time spent on reviewing contracts and other legal documents, improving efficiency.

2. **Increased Accuracy**: The AI system was able to flag potentially problematic clauses and offer suggestions with greater accuracy than traditional manual review.

3. **Cost Savings**: Law firms and corporate legal departments were able to reduce the need for large teams of junior associates to handle routine tasks, allowing lawyers to focus on higher-value work.

Challenges and Solutions:

- **Model Interpretability**: Legal professionals required transparency into the system's decision-making process. The team developed an explanation feature that provided clear rationales for the system's recommendations.

- **Data Privacy**: Given the sensitive nature of legal documents, the platform used end-to-end encryption and ensured compliance with data protection regulations.

Conclusion:

LLMs have significantly improved the efficiency and accuracy of legal document analysis and research, helping legal professionals save time and reduce costs.

Case Study 5: LLMs in Customer Insights: Sentiment Analysis for Brand Management

Overview:

In the field of brand management, companies rely heavily on customer feedback and sentiment analysis to shape their strategies. LLMs are being used to process and analyze social media, customer reviews, and surveys to gain insights into consumer sentiment and behavior.

Challenge:

Traditional sentiment analysis models often struggle with understanding nuanced language, sarcasm, and domain-specific expressions in customer feedback. As a result, companies were unable to extract meaningful insights from large volumes of data, leading to missed opportunities for brand improvement.

Implementation:

A global consumer goods company adopted LLMs to improve its sentiment analysis capabilities. By fine-tuning an LLM on a corpus of customer reviews, social media posts, and product feedback, the company developed a system that could accurately detect sentiment in text, including subtle nuances, sarcasm, and mixed emotions.

Key steps included:

1. **Data Collection**: The LLM was trained on a large and diverse dataset of customer reviews, tweets,

and forum discussions related to the company's products.

2. **Sentiment Analysis**: The LLM was fine-tuned to classify text into positive, negative, or neutral sentiments while also detecting mixed emotions and sarcasm.

3. **Real-Time Feedback**: The system was integrated with the company's social media monitoring tools to provide real-time sentiment analysis of ongoing campaigns.

Outcome:

The LLM-powered sentiment analysis system led to:

1. **Better Consumer Insights**: The company gained a deeper understanding of customer

perceptions, allowing it to tailor marketing strategies and product features to customer desires.

2. **Crisis Management**: By detecting negative sentiment early, the company was able to quickly respond to customer concerns and prevent potential PR crises.

3. **Improved Customer Engagement**: The brand used insights from sentiment analysis to engage customers more effectively through targeted communications.

Challenges and Solutions:

- **Handling Sarcasm**: The model initially struggled with sarcasm and irony in customer feedback.

To address this, the system was fine-tuned on a specialized dataset of sarcastic statements.

- **Data Privacy**: The company ensured customer data was anonymized and used only for sentiment analysis in compliance with privacy laws.

Conclusion:

LLMs are transforming brand management by providing more accurate and nuanced sentiment analysis, helping companies better understand and engage their customers.

Chapter 9: The Road Ahead: What to Expect from Future LLMs

The LLM landscape is constantly evolving, and the future holds exciting possibilities. This chapter explores some key trends to watch for:

- **Advancements in LLM Capabilities:**

  - **Increased Accuracy and Fluency:** LLMs will continue to learn and improve, generating more accurate and natural-sounding language.

  - **Enhanced Reasoning and Understanding:** Future LLMs might be able to reason more logically and develop a deeper understanding of the world around them.

  - **Learning from Different Modalities:** Imagine LLMs that can not only process text but also learn from images, audio, and other forms of data, leading to a more holistic understanding of information.

- **Integration of LLMs with Other AI Technologies:** The future belongs to collaboration! Imagine LLMs working seamlessly with other AI technologies like computer vision and robotics. This could lead to the development of even more sophisticated intelligent systems capable of performing complex tasks in the real world.

- **The Evolving Role of Humans in the LLM Era:** LLMs are not designed to replace humans; they are here to augment our capabilities. As LLMs take over routine tasks, humans can focus on creative endeavors, strategic thinking, and tasks that require social intelligence and emotional understanding. The key will be to find a balance

between human and machine intelligence,

leveraging the strengths of both for optimal

results.

Chapter 10: Conclusion: Embracing the Potential of

Large Language Models

Large Language Models are powerful tools with the potential to revolutionize various aspects of our lives. By understanding their capabilities, limitations, and ethical considerations, we can harness the power of LLMs for good. As we move forward, it's crucial to develop LLMs responsibly, ensuring they are unbiased, transparent, and used for positive societal impact.

This book has equipped you with the foundation to navigate the exciting world of LLMs. Remember, the future is what we make it, and LLMs can be powerful partners in shaping a better tomorrow. Let's embrace the potential of these models and work together to ensure they are developed and used ethically and responsibly.

www.ingramcontent.com/pod-product-compliance
Lightning Source LLC
La Vergne TN
LVHW051659050326
832903LV00032B/3898